Gathering Advertising

You want to play out a quest for the specialty discussion that accommodates your showcasing needs.

Ordered Advertisements

- CraigsList - http://www.craigslist.com
- USFreeAds - http://www.usfreeads.com
- Backpage - http://www.backpage.com
- Kijiji - http://www.kijiji.com
- Oodle - http://www.oodle.com

Long range interpersonal communication Destinations

- Facbook - http://www.facbook.com
- Twitter - http://www.twitter.com
- Yippee Gatherings - http://groups.yahoo.com
- MySpace - http://www.myspace.com
- Ning - http://www.ning.com

Pay Per Snap Promoting

Google Adwords - http://adwords.google.com
Yippee Search - http://searchmarketing.yahoo.com

Microsoft - http://advertising.microsoft.com

Deal, Lead or Snap

Member networks are intended to repay their partners in view of 3 distinct sorts of activities: pay per click (PPC), pay per lead (PPL), and pay per deal (PPS).

Pay Per Snap

Pay Per Snap implies when a guest to a site page taps on an offshoot connect, the partner procures a specific sum.

All the guest needs to do is navigate and see the commercial - it requires no other sort of activity for the member to get compensated.

PPC is generally the least paying sort of activity, yet the most straightforward to finish.

Pay Per Lead

A guest taps on an offshoot connection and finishes up a structure mentioning more data, joining a pamphlet or online gathering.

PPL for the most part doesn't need a money exchange or Visa data.

Pay Per Deal

Pay Per Deal is typically the most lucrative kind of activity. It additionally is the hardest (for the most part) to finish.

In PPS, the guest should finish a buy or enter their Visa to take part in an item or preliminary deal.

The Workmanship and Business of Member Showcasing (Affiliate marketing)

The member gets a rate (commission) of the deal.

"Two-Level and Three - Level" Member Projects

Member programs are two-level projects that convey commissions in view of a reference organization of recruits and sub-partners. As you might have advanced at this point with LeadLock we have made one of a handful of the 3 level member programs!

Model: Member A signs up to an offshoot program and gets compensated for a deal or lead by a guest.

!

The Workmanship and Business of Member Showcasing (Affiliate marketing)

What is Member Showcasing? (Affiliate marketing)

Member showcasing is a kind of promoting where an individual advances someone else's item or administration and makes a commission from every deal. The partner advertiser has no responsibilities regarding the item quality, conveyance or upkeep of item - other than the ethical obligation to their clients of advancing results of high worth to them.

Why partake in Member Showcasing? (Affiliate marketing)

Member promoting permits you the valuable chance to work part-time or full time while building a liberal lingering pay.

"Leftover pay (likewise called detached or repeating pay) is pay that keeps on being created after the underlying exertion is consumed." - Marty Foley

Member advertising is perhaps of the most straightforward strategy I am aware of to bring in cash with next to zero startup costs and very little innovation information required.

There are additionally viable low-to-no spending plan showcasing strategies accessible -- the item proprietor is doing the significant promoting to acquire item or administration openness.

Subsidiary promoting is something you can begin promptly while you're figuring out how to make your own items and sites.

Subsidiary showcasing is an income creating action that you can do while you fabricate your fundamental Web benefit stream

Offshoot Advancement Cycle

Underneath you will see another stream outline I have assembled so that you that helps you might see the fundamental Associate Advertising stream process that you will be engaged with during your Offshoot Promoting.

Create paypal account < find products with affiliates program < sign up as an affiliate < mask your affiliate URL
< market the product or service < receive your commissions < repeat the process

Familiar Ways Of advancing Associate Items

As of now I'm about to show a few extraordinary ways that I feel you could focus on to advance your subsidiary items when you are simply starting your Member Promoting adventure. In the accompanying pages we will delve into additional subtleties on the ones that I feel would be best for a novice to get everything rolling with.

List Advancements By fostering a relationship with your rundown, you can advance things that you feel would be important to them.

Contributing to a blog Publishing content to a blog is one more unbelievable method for advancing subsidiary items. Paid sites, where you buy and host your own space, are the best. In any case, there are free options that can likewise be powerful.

A few locales where you can set up a free blog:

! Blogger Blog - http://www.blogger.com

! WordPress - http://www.wordpress.com

! Weebly - http://www.weebly.com

! Virtual Entertainment Showcasing

! HubPages - http://www.hubpages.com

The Workmanship and Business of Member Showcasing (Affiliate marketing)

! Squidoo - http://www.squidoo.com Article Promoting
! Ezine Articles - http://www.ezinearticles.com

! Go Articles - http://www.goarticles.com/

! Article Dashboard - http://articledashboard.com

! Simple Articles - http://www.easyarticles.com Video Showcasing (item surveys/benefits)
! YouTube - http://www.youtube.com

! Genuine Individuals - http://www.realpeoplerealstuff.com

! Revver - http://www.revver.com

! MySpace Video - http://vids.myspace.com/

!

!

!

On the off chance that Member A draws in Partner B to pursue a similar program utilizing his sign-up code (or associate code), Offshoot B turns into a sub-partner of Partner A. Presently Subsidiary B draws in a partner - he is currently getting the essential member commission and An is getting commissions on both B and C - lovely cool!

Tracking down Items to Advance

At the point when you are searching for items to advance there are a few fundamental variables you ought to be thinking about when you are searching for items.

Likewise think about a portion of the accompanying proposals when you prescribe an item to your rundown or as a Subsidiary for any item.

! Be fastidious about what you advance, and get some margin to be certain that all that you suggest is of real worth.

!   Be Straightforward while making your proposals! Nothing will dismiss individuals more rapidly than an explicit endeavor to fill them brimming with publicity and hot air to make sure you can make a couple of fast bucks.

!   Get some margin to go through the item early on to know precisely exact thing you are advancing and that it is really worth the worth you are attempting to sell somebody on.

(Particularly in the event that it is an Advertiser you don't know well overall, and you are curious about the nature of item they convey.)

! You ought not be selling what you don't put stock in and, the truth of the matter is simply private

tributes will do a ton to support your deals.

Deciding Elements of Associate Items

A portion of the normal inquiries posed by member advertisers are these.

What item would it be advisable for me to sell as a subsidiary?

What offshoot items are hot selling?

Straightforward: Exploration is the main arrangement here.

The Needs are the deciding aspects among numerous decisions.

The Need-Needs are the fundamental reasons an individual is searching for the item or administration.

The Worth Driver-Worth Drivers are the qualities or intangibles related with an item or administration. They are entirely of "needs" yet your worth drivers will turn out to be critical when items or administrations are not separated from other comparative items being advertised.

Coming up next are three incredible spots to find items that you can turn into a partner for:

The Workmanship and Business of Member Showcasing (Affiliate marketing)

http://www.clickbank.com
http://www.paydotcom.com

Commission Intersection http://www.cj.com Different spots to consider evaluating:
! http://www.click2sell.eu/

! http://www.shareasale.com/!

http://amazon.com

Elements to Consider While Picking an Item to Advance

There are many variables to consider while choosing a member program to advance. Here are only a portion of the elements that you ought to be searching for while settling on what subsidiary items to advance. !   Pertinence: Advance projects that supplement the subject of your site or your Specialty.

o Guests are now intrigued by the subject of our site, provides you with the benefit of a simpler deals change.

!   Quality and Solidness: There is a tremendous amount of Partner Items, don't Make due with a program that is messy just to have an item to advance..

!

!

!

o Search for good trustworthy organizations that are steady. o Request to address existing partners

o Ensure that full contact subtleties are given.

! Commissions: To the extent that commission rates go, search for items that you will procure a base commission of $20.
o o o o

To accomplish greatest benefits, I suggest that you go for the gold the half - 100 percent level. Top of the line item will generally be lower commissions 25%-half

Lifetime Commissions. (your client you sent is cookied to you forever)

Lingering Commission

When are commissions paid

! Associate Help: The best organizations to work with give a lot of help

o Limited time material accessible: example advertisements, pennants, logos

o Exhortation about boosting deals gave.

o Insights on navigate deals and income ought to be given and refreshed consistently.

o Ready to get your inquiries responded to in a sensible timeframe - say, in 24 hours or less. Be sensible. In the event that an item proprietor is in a center of a significant send off his help will commonly be heavier and they might be somewhat behind.

Deals Page or the Pitch Page

! View pitch page to assist you with diving deeper into the item and get thoughts on the most proficient The Workmanship and Business of Member Showcasing (Affiliate marketing) method to advance it, for example, what catchphrases individuals could look to find it, benefits you can

feature in your advancements, and the sky is the limit from there.

! Search for items with great deals page to showcase as an offshoot

! Is there a decent solid and Infectious title

! Is deals page text or video deals page

! Is deals page spotless and simple to explore

! Great substantial, strong, authentic tributes from genuine individuals!

! Is there a decent solid clear source of inspiration

! Does deals page have releases that will ransack your payments

Cautioning - search for deals page "spills"

As a partner you believe the guest should peruse the business page and hit that request button with you getting credit for the deal. There are various justifications for why this doesn't occur. We call these breaks in the deals page.

! Connection to an offshoot join page. Your potential client could just turn into a subsidiary and buy (take your bonus) the item himself.

! Item Proprietor offers various installment choices so for instance in the event that you are utilizing a ClickBank ID and ClickBank isn't picked you may not get the commission.

! The item you are advancing is only one of numerous inconsequential items on a page - a set aside for the expected client.

! There are numerous outside joins which occupy the guest from arriving at the request page.

! The item proprietor catches your bonus.

There are offers to join a mailing rundown or guarantee a free report: More often than not you will get credited for any deal resulting from these leads however once in a while you might stumble into a corrupt item proprietor that might follow up and make the deal through his own connection.

Connect Shrouding

!

One of the basic activities as a subsidiary advertiser is to safeguard your pay potential.

By covering or shrouding your connection you can safeguard your Partner ID and your offshoot payments.

The following are a couple of spots you can look into to assist you with veiling your subsidiary connection and assist you with safeguarding your member bonuses.

- Tie.ly - http://Tie.ly (My undisputed top choice)

  Power Connection Generator (Mike Filsaime Item)
  Cli.gs - http://www.cli.gs/

  Uforgot.me - http://www.uforgot.me/

- BudURL - http://budurl.com/

So Many Subsidiary Projects! Which One Do I Pick?

The Workmanship and Business of Member Showcasing (Affiliate marketing)

At the point when you begin searching for a definitive member program to go along with you will find that you will be confronted with many prospects wherever you look. Picking the compose Member program can be a major piece of the achievement you accomplish as a Subsidiary Advertiser.

Here are a few things you ought to take a gander at to assist you with pursuing the best choice.

- Will it cost you anything to join? Out of the hundreds and thousands of Subsidiary projects accessible to you to browse my suggestion

is to avoid those requesting that you pay. There are a lot of free projects for you to browse which will give you great outcomes.

- When do they give the commission checks?

Knowing when you will accept your bonuses is generally something worth being thankful for to find out.

Some will pay you immediately after a deal and others will stand by 30 days or after discount periods are over to pay your bonuses.

Realizing this data will assist you with arranging Deals Page or the Pitch Page

- View pitch page to assist you with studying the item and get thoughts on the most proficient method to advance it, for example, what watchwords individuals could look to find it, benefits you can feature in your advancements, and that's just the beginning.

- Search for items with great deals page to showcase as a partner

- Is there a decent solid and Snappy title

- Is deals page text or video deals page

- Is deals page perfect and simple to explore

- Great substantial, strong, genuine tributes from genuine individuals!

- Is there a decent solid clear source of inspiration

- Does deals page have releases that will loot

your bonuses

-

Cautioning - search for deals page "spills"

As a partner you believe the guest should peruse the business page and hit that request button with you getting credit for the deal. There are various justifications for why this doesn't occur. We call these breaks in the deals page.

! Connection to a subsidiary sign up page. Your potential client could basically turn into an associate and buy (take your bonus) the item himself.

! Item Proprietor offers various installment choices so for instance in the event that you are utilizing a ClickBank ID and ClickBank isn't picked you may not get the commission.

! The item you are advancing is only one of numerous irrelevant items on a page - a set aside for the possible client.

! There are numerous outer connections which divert the guest from arriving at the request page.

! The item proprietor catches your bonus. There are offers to join a mailing rundown or guarantee a free

The Workmanship and Business of Member Showcasing (Affiliate marketing)

report: More often than not you will get credited for any deal resulting from these leads yet once in a while you might stumble into a deceitful item proprietor that might follow up and make the deal through his own connection.

Connect Shrouding

One of the basic activities as a partner advertiser is to safeguard your pay potential.

By covering or shrouding your connection you can safeguard your Associate ID and your partner bonuses.

The following are a couple of spots you can look into to assist you with covering your member connection and help you p your own monetary financial plans.

! What are the transformation rates? Realizing the change rates for the items you are elevating will assist you with checking whether your outcomes from the endeavors are in accordance with others you have advanced. It will assist you with choosing if the item merits advancing in any case.

On the off chance that you are getting lower change rates contrasted with different advertisers it might mean you really want to increase the special determination on your end. Utilize the transformations as a rule to keep for your own endeavors.

In the event that you are getting extensive lower than most different offshoots you might need to ask the item proprietor what has worked for others in advancing their items.

!   Does this program have a lot of instruments and assets? Finding Member programs which give legitimate devices to advancing the item will be a major assistance to you in your advancing endeavors.

Commonly you might see there are no apparatuses accessible for you to use during your advancement. Feel free to inquire as to whether they can give these instruments to help.

Commonly they simply have been occupied and neglected to get them stacked up to the apparatuses pages.
Numerous different times they simply never considered it yet would love to essentially furnish you with some great swipe duplicate or standard advertisements to assist you with better advancing their item.

!   How are references from a member's site followed and for how long do they stay in the framework?

!   What are the sorts of member details accessible?

Many Offshoot projects will give you reports which you can follow taps on your connections, deals you made and your change rate, and so on. These are critical to be aware so you can monitor your special endeavors and have a superior comprehension with respect to what is happening and roll out any improvements expected to obtain improved results.

!   Does the partner program pay for the hits and impressions, other than the commissions on deals?

!   Who are you working with? (Is it actually a strong organization?) By all means you ought to research any business you are going to become engaged with as a Subsidiary advertiser. It is critical to know who you are working with and what sort of notoriety they have. Carve out opportunity to do all necessary investigation early on before you end up consumed by somebody with a not exactly decent standing.

!   Is the subsidiary a one-level or two-level program? The contrast between the one and two level program is the two levels, you will get made up for any commissions created by different Partners you allude to the Subsidiary program.

!   Is this a program you like and have interest ready? In the event that it doesn't energize and intrigue you how might you be at effectively advancing the item? You really want your interest group to feel your excitement and interest over the item you advance for them to feel it is something critical to them too.

The Workmanship and Business of Member Showcasing (Affiliate marketing)

!	Is ideal for your designated crowd? You won't find lasting success at advancing items your objective market isn't keen on.

I'm certain this is an easy decision for most perusing this book !

!	Ultimately, what is how much commission paid? I think this one justifies itself. Ensure you understand what sort of commissions you are

buckling down for. My proposal is to not engage with commissions under half except if it is for high ticket things.

Utilizing Item Proposals to Build Your Primary concern

Item proposal is one of the best ways of advancing a Subsidiary item.

On the off chance that clients trust you, they will trust your suggestions.

Suggest items you genuinely trust. Those you are prescribing items to will detect the certainty you have in some random item.

Give a decent item survey.
Make sure to specify things you could do without about items during your survey.

You should be mindful so as to not make the item strong like it is actually a terrible item.

Assuming the item truly has an excessive number of awful things you will remember for your survey I would avoid it.

Likewise be cautious in the event that you are doing a survey as in not suggesting an item.

Be mindful so as not to tear an item a section in a manner to lessen the validity of the item proprietor.

There are more viable ways of overtaking your opposition than to attempt to destroy them.

I have said this multiple occasions and I will say it by and by,

"Just advance items which match your interest group and satisfy the requirements and needs they have."

KNOW YOUR Clients.

Advance items which position well in your item channel.

It should sound good to the client before they buy.

You might have to return and peruse making and situating your powerful proposition on the off chance that you are don't know regarding what I'm referring to this moment.

Getting Yourself Seen on the Subsidiary Promoting Radar

Perhaps of the best thing you can achieve as a Partner advertiser is to get yourself and your endeavors saw by the advertisers you are advancing for.

This opens up a wide range of chances to you which you might struggle with before, for example, finding JV accomplices to help advance and develop your own business.

The following are the main 4 different ways I feel you can approach getting seen on the Member radar.

1. Assemble your rundown.

The Workmanship and Business of Member Showcasing (Affiliate marketing)

This is tremendous for yourself as well as your Member development in such countless ways.

Not in the least does having a bigger and more responsive rundown assist you with creating more deals as a Partner, yet additionally once you have a laid out list which is working for yourself and developing you can use this rundown in getting others on your side to start helping you. It doesn't stay confidential for extremely lengthy who the advertisers are with great responsive rundown.

2. Set up a good foundation for yourself as a Super-Offshoot. Go above and beyond in your Associate endeavors to become taken note. Really buckle down a realizing all you can to become one of the top Subsidiaries in your field.

Make sure to put yourself out there to be seen. Really bend over backward to lay out your presence in any capacity you can.

3. Drive your own in-interest item. Driving your own in interest items give you the validity you want to ascend to the highest point of your Subsidiary endeavors.
Many individuals will get into Associate Showcasing on the grounds that they feel it gets them far from being required to make their own items.

I feel this is the kind of thing which couldn't possibly be more off-base. On the off chance that you will be prescribing items it just makes sense you must have validity and be viewed as a specialist in your Specialty to acquire the regard and trust from those you are prescribing items to.

Making your own items additionally offers you something to propose as a trade off when the item proprietor of the Subsidiary items you are advancing sees the incredible work you have been doing and asks you how the individual can help you.

Decide to not make your own items is just overlooking heaps of cash for different Partners and item proprietors to gather totally free from you.

4. Foster associations with different advertisers.

Again this is putting your-self out there to be seen. Bend over backward to construct solid connections and let others see you are hoping to work effectively and ready to learn.

Show them you fully intend to take care of business and plan to remain for the long stretch. It is difficult to assemble associations with somebody just to have them drop off the planet after some time and not heard from once more.

Member Showcasing the Adaptation Condition

There is a sure request which must be followed in the event that you are really going to find lasting success at being an Offshoot Advertiser.

It isn't simply snatching a subsidiary connection for any old member item and hope to make a lot of cash.

Indeed it is feasible to bring in cash with this technique yet it isn't the strategy the solid Partners use to make enormous amounts of money.

Everything begins with "YOU" giving an answer for an issue through Incredible Substance...

Your substance is found by those scanning on the web for the answer for the issue you have found them having through your legitimate exploration.

This is known as your traffic.

When your traffic runs into you due to you being strategically set up to meet them, you start the Pre-sell process which is made through the relationship and all the more great strong substance which you exceed expectations to the guest.

The Workmanship and Business of Member Showcasing (Affiliate marketing)

Then, at that point, and really at that time, comes adaptation

Content...

The Issue Solver

Online guests search for Content.

They are not searching for you! (Basically they don't realize they are yet)

Guests don't have any acquaintance with you, and most couldn't care less about you.

They are centered around answers for their concerns or needs as a matter of some importance.

You want to stand apart over the group and be the one they find! In the event that you don't... you fizzle! There are two or three vital things you really want to recall with regards to the substance you are giving.

! Situating yourself accurately before your guests over your opposition.

! Separate yourself from your opposition.

Put forth a valiant effort to convey extraordinary substance which, most importantly, tackles your guests issues.

Thusly you will assemble Extraordinary Traffic, which offers you the chance to be Pre-sold.

Then and really at that time, are you prepared to Adapt.

You want to begin all along not at the ideal outcome.

Try not to resemble such countless individuals who initially invest investment setting up a shopping basket and a trader record or another approach to "gathering the cash.

Transform information into content.

Then, at that point, convert your substance into pay.

Traffic Age

A developing Subsidiary Business should have Traffic to appropriately get by.

On the off chance that you don't have traffic to the substance the adaptation interaction won't happen.

Traffic is viewed as by numerous the soul of any on the web or disconnected business.

A web-based business is the same than a disconnected business without traffic.

Obviously you additionally need the right sort of traffic for adaptation to happen appropriately too.

With no site traffic, your site won't make you any cash or create any leads.

As anyone might expect, a great many people don't have the foggiest idea about this.

They wrongly trust in the "Form it and they will come" rule thinking they simply need to fabricate a site and traffic will consequently run to it.

This is totally off-base. Furthermore, thus, a few sites turn out to be deserted. Albeit a few irregular guests will go over your site, the reality remains… critical lucrative traffic doesn't simply show up.

The Workmanship and Business of Member Showcasing (Affiliate marketing)

Begin with one road first and expert this road of traffic prior to continuing on toward new techniques.

Commonly new Associate advertisers will get so up to speed in attempting to produce numerous roads of traffic they never truly improve at any of them and their endeavors stay stale.

Pre-selling for Offshoot Adaptation

Pre-Selling is situating your proposal in the brain of the guest so it's a good idea to purchase!

The greatest thing you need to recollect is that you are managing a total outsider, and you are a finished outsider to your new guest.

They don't have any acquaintance with you, similar to you, or trust you YET! Until the guest meets you at your site they have no method for laying out a relationship with you yet.

Pre-selling is an ideal opportunity to assemble guest trust in you... (The trust factor) How? By Exceeding expectations... Exceeding expectations is the point at which you go past what your client was guaranteed or at any point anticipated... your guests will "LOVE" you.

(Except if you as of now have a major brand name like Amazon, Quick "selling" on Sites is insufficient.)

List assemble is vital to your general showcasing and it means quite a bit to your pre-selling endeavors. Getting an individual on your rundown gives you the high ground and places you in charge and offers you more preselling open doors.

Two or three these pre-selling open doors you have accessible to you are

!   Follow Up email series

!   Online classes, Teleseminars, Broadcast messages

These techniques are perfect to keep on conveying more satisfied and worth to additional your preselling to those not sold at the site.

Adaptation Interaction of Associate Showcasing

Out of the relative multitude of steps we take care of I would need to say that adaptation is the simple aspect.

All that you have instituted whenever done appropriately will prompt adaptation.

In the event that you go through every one of the last 3 stages nevertheless are not seeing any sort of adaptation, you really want to return and investigate how you veered off-track in the initial 3 stages.

Your Partner item suggestions (if all around picked and situated) ought to offer an extra support and offer valued benefit for your guests who will thusly compensate you when they open their wallet and reward you!

(You have now adapted)

The member model is an incredible income source.

(It generally seems OK to add Partner Promoting as an incredible type of revenue into your business. I suggest that you generally differentiate your pay sources.)

A vital piece of the adaptation interaction for you to acknowledge is that, adaptation is where you presently have some control. Up until this point the guest was in finished control.

They could leave and you could at no point ever see or hear from them in the future and lose the chance to offer more benefit and make further deals.

Content Blog Partner Promoting

Making specialty locales as well as sites can be an extraordinary choice for subsidiaries who have additional time and imagination than cash.

Assuming you are searching for some technique for Member Showcasing that conveys moment results I need to express front and center this isn't so much for you. Like article advertising, this strategy can take time before you begin getting results, so it's not something you ought to hope to show quick returns.

It is anyway an extraordinary method for making supportable long haul benefits, and an incredible validity developer with at least cash spent. Think consistency!

In the same way as other different parts of web based promoting consistency is the way to Partner Showcasing through a substance blog.

Cost for making your own self-facilitated blog;

!   Space name and facilitating, yet these are normally little. $20-$50 to get everything rolling.

!   Little month to month for facilitating. For the most part under $20 per month.

In spite of the fact that I don't suggest the free choice for your expert blog, there are numerous choices to get your own webpage or blog that is facilitated free of charge.

Downsides of a free blog are, you might be more restricted on choices like, the look and feel of the webpage, the number of pages your website that can have, your adaptation might be restricted if by any means, and control of content, and a major Validity destroyer!

Be extremely cautious purchasing instant locales... these locales might have restricted works like Website design enhancement!

Plan Well and Stay on course

Plans for adaptation of your substance blog expect you to design well and adhere to your arrangement. The hardest work is toward the beginning. The principal deal is consistently the hardest and generally expensive to get!

Publishing content to a blog gets more straightforward whenever you have gathered speed.

Be Steady!

When you have energy taking a different path is hard

Ponder your ongoing readership... Will they acknowledge the change? Assuming you have perusers that are perusing your blog for how you are presently, you need to think about that reality that they probably won't generally approve of the new changes and escape.

For the most part altering your perspective means beginning once again and once again working without any preparation. B heading in a different direction mid-stream implies a ton of lost time and torment!

The Significant Initial feeling

New guests show up at your blog regularly as more satisfied is created and advanced. What is the guests vital Initial feeling?

The present moment they are just a guest that is a likely client. They are not acquainted with you or with the publicizing, or content on your blog, and further more they couldn't care less about you. (However)

We should investigate a few things that will assist you with making an extraordinary initial feeling for your new blog guest to keep them needing to return endlessly time once more.

! Keep your site straightforward and clean, and simple to explore!

The Workmanship and Business of Member Showcasing (Affiliate marketing)

!	It's not time for gaudy pennants and purchase presently fastens.

Everything really revolves around building a relationship with individuals through your substance and your image.

My number one saying right now is, "on the grounds that you can doesn't mean you ought to!"

Simply pause for a minute to contemplate what I recently said and I figure it will soak in regarding what I'm referring to.

!	Give great significant Specialty explicit, critical thinking content. Recollect that the reason for content is to offer some benefit to other people. Do you offer real benefit, and is it the best you're equipped for giving?

When you gain guest trust and love in what you give them you can gradually start to adapt them. Takes time and commitment, and consistency, yet to peruse then different income streams open up !   Never accept that your site guest thinks often about you or your item!

Your guest takes one glance at your site and pivots and leaves.... Why?

You planned your site for your necessities, not their requirements.

Here is something surprisingly more dreadful to ponder; after they pass on they're going to one of your rivals' locales and purchase something.

What guests care about when they make an appearance to your site is, does the substance tackle their concerns?

Several things to get on paper and spot where you can consider them to be your structure your site:

!	The main explanation my site exists is to tackle my clients' concerns.

!	What issues do the page and the substance I'm making tackle?

!	Make it clear to your guests what your blog/website is about.

Try not to misdirect them!

Assuming you need improved results stop the whole showing of knife little deceives. You believe that your guest should find precisely exact thing they came looking for.

Try not to utilize minimal dispensable substance just to increment site hits and promotion impressions.

Your objective ought to be to genuinely help you guest that makes an appearance to your blog, and my conviction is that whatever else is burning through their experience as well as the time you spent adding it to your website.

I find that content rich articles that truly give a meat to the guest are better at producing connections and references and building traffic.

Make the most of initial feelings. You believe the guest should feel like the visit to your site was time all around spent, and that the guest leaves feeling they partook in some serious detract from the substance you gave.

The Workmanship and Business of Member Showcasing (Affiliate marketing)

Your Composing Style Matters

The style wherein you compose your blog entries can incredibly influence the readership of your blog.

Compose as though you actually know every individual who is perusing your blog.

My idea is to constantly be pursuing structure a relationship with your perusers so they believe they "know" you.

By setting aside some margin for them to get to know you, and by you getting to know your perusers, you will foster a dependable peruser base for your blog.

Watch out... Think Tenable Master Versus Fellowships

Show that you give it a second thought, and are keen on your perusers.

This will foster dependability and even assist your blog with becoming famous online .

This not just brings you more perusers it eventually gives more Subsidiary Connection Navigate.

Take a gander at your Blog Entries according to the viewpoint of your perusers.

Understand them!

Making Your Blog Content

In this next segment I will talk about 4 methods for producing extraordinary substance that will assist you in the adaptation with handling of your writing for a blog endeavors.

1. Compose it yourself-Best technique... after all you are the expert...Your character is something to be thankful for to be found in your work. Downside is that it is tedious on your part.

2. Re-appropriating You can finish short blog entries for about $2-10 at www.Articlez.com , ODesk.com, Fighter Gathering, and so on...

! Search for essayists who have major areas of strength for a. Request important composing tests like the kind of article thinking of you want done. Understand them... In the event that you need your Blog entries to rank well, ensure they will be composed for perusers as a matter of some importance..

! Continuously take a look at the substance to guarantee it is what you need and that it is great strong substance. Try not to acknowledge poo.

! Request articles not blog entries. Most will charge more in the event that you say you want a blog entry composed.

Masters and Cons To Re-appropriating Benefits (Professionals):

o You don't need to invest energy doing the exploration

o The time you save in having another person do your composing is time you can spend showcasing

o The expense is insignificant

o It's normally proficient and incredibly quick

o You typically can pay solely after you support the work.

Weaknesses (Cons) :

o The essayist probably won't consent to your terms (Continue to look) o The author might take more time than they or you expected o The author may not compose English easily, ! !

The Workmanship and Business of Member Showcasing (Affiliate marketing)

o You might wind up with a novice rather than proficient author.

o The essayist may not be as knowledgeable about Website design enhancement as need might arise

o The author might be incredible at Website design enhancement, however not be truly adept at composing for individuals

3. Visitor Writing for a blog

Exchange posting blog happy with another blogger is designated "visitor contributing to a blog."

One thing to constantly recall is that, the more your blog, the more visitor open doors you will have!

!	Search for Online journals that don't straightforwardly contend with one another for perusers, when you do you can turn into an additional support of one another and to our separate perusers.

!	Your blog may essentially be on work at home open doors and bringing in cash on the web so you could find another Blog that has to do with something almost identical or with an interest group that might want to catch wind of home lucrative open doors like a Blog that arrangements with Stay at home guardians.

!	You trade "visitor" posts… You compose content on that Blog with a byline and interface (back-connect) back to my own Blog

!	The proprietor of the Stay at home guardians blog composes content on your Blog with a byline and connect (back-interface) back to their own Blog

!	You presently approach the devoted perusers of another blog and they will approach your blog..

4. Confidential Mark Privileges Content (PLR)

Utilizing Private Mark freedoms items or PLR is one of my unsurpassed most loved approaches to creating and tracking down satisfied for my substance websites.

! Advantages of PLR

o Life hack - Who couldn't need additional opportunity in their day? Composing, despite the fact that extremely worth the effort, can take a lot of time. That time could be better spent somewhere else.

o Modest - PLR is more straightforward on the wallet. Who could do without that! ! o Adaptability - Rework it, add your own twist and character

o Productive - Transform into Blog Entries with your Partner Connections

! Zero in on PLR reports and Books specifically.

o Not at all like PLR articles, confidential name privileges reports make reusing

your substance considerably more straightforward. Get the most value for your money.

Offshoot Connections in your Blog Entries

One of the best adaptation techniques is to add decisively positioned and applicable subsidiary connects to your destinations.

One of the best subsidiary connections can be

found inside the text of your blog entry.

You might be imagining that no one needs to make an appearance to your blog and be pitched at the entire time they are perusing your blog. That is some savvy thinking on your part. Your work recorded as a hard copy

The Workmanship and Business of Member Showcasing (Affiliate marketing)

isn't to pitch, it is to presell and lead them to the source of inspiration point of your post. With the expanded utilization of sites you will observe that blog perusers are accustomed to seeing connections in blog entries.

However long the connection has importance for being there, prompts a significant advantage for the peruser, and offers an answer for their concern or need, you won't insult anybody and you will end up with a higher

navigate… a navigate will frequently prompt a deal.

What I just said is something vital.

Pre-sell the navigate on your Member Connection through your substance.

As somebody peruses your substance they need to feel they are getting some genuine worth and help. Try not to pitch an item

Your responsibility is to pre-sell the item, and inspire them to make a move by tapping on your offshoot connect that you have decisively positioned all through your post.

The following two or three things to recall while composing your substance for your post;

! Show sympathy (understanding and going into another's sentiments) with your peruser's circumstance or issue.

!   Offer a Member item or administration that will furnish them with a reasonable answer for their concern. Try not to misjudge the force of partner joins when your proposal arrives at thousands day to day. Adaptation through Blog Audits

Blog Audits

On the off chance that you have a rundown of endorsers you will find that occasionally email content is sufficiently not to pre-sell your item proposal.

Once in a while all that's needed is somewhat more of a push and an extraordinary method for doing so is to guide your guests to a Blog Surveys Website where you will actually want to give somewhat more meat to your proposal.

Individuals may not be open minded toward a tedious email where they will hope to see somewhat more happy being conveyed through your post on your blog.

There are a couple of truly cool advantages of utilizing the blog survey technique.

!   With a blog survey you can give item pictures, insert a video survey, and by and large deal more happy to pre-sell the offers.

!   Blog surveys permit you to get traffic from the web crawlers assuming you utilize the title of the item in the title of the post.

! You can interface with your rundown from a blog survey. Send them to your blog to peruse your survey.

This starts preparing your perusers t make a move rather than simply perusing your messages. Make sure to express the undeniable while composing you're survey.

Try not to underrate how little your peruser may really be aware of the subject or item you are looking into. There's compelling reason need to give a full biography, however a touch of foundation data is in every case great.

The Workmanship and Business of Member Showcasing (Affiliate marketing)

Be explicit Model: Live occasion survey... Make sense of the air of the occasion, the participant's response to specific speakers, how the hosts preformed, the worth of the substance educated, specific focuses that truly hung out in the speaker's substance, and so on.

Your special selling point

Numerous an advertiser is attempting to get some additional money by getting on the blog survey cart and many fall flat and never make a dime. One reason many neglect to at any point prevail with a blog survey is on the grounds that they are offering nothing not the same as any other individual. Ponder having a "exceptional selling point" something that your survey can offer that individuals will not have the option to find somewhere else.

o Do you figure out how to carry a clever inclination to it?

o Do you have a particular or intriguing mastery about the subject

o Is your viewpoint immeasurably unique to that of every other person?

o Have you figured out how to be the first to audit something?

Utilize your own singular uniqueness that you have for your potential benefit. Your spotlight isn't just on the item you are checking on, it is additionally on your uniqueness and why somebody ought to pay attention to you over top of every other person around.

Try not to simply expound on yourself.

Be cautious while discussing your uniqueness. When you have them snared in get off of yourself being the current subject. All in all ensure that you don't expound on yourself. Commentators need to be aware of the item, and that ought to be what you focus on.

While composing your blog survey the main inquiry going through your head ought to be, "what is it that the peruser need to be aware?" This is overwhelmingly significant to recall while composing a survey.

You can create the wittiest survey with the cleverest illustrations, yet except if the peruser figures out what they need to be aware, you've not taken care of your business as a commentator.

Put forth a valiant effort to consider the kind of inquiries your readership is probably going to get some information about the item or administration you are investigating.

For the most part I find that the inquiries I have going through my head, are relatively close from what my perusers need to be aware too.

Be Straightforward

In the event that you compose a Blog surveys, as per the FTC rules and guidelines, you need to unveil assuming you are being repaid by a maker, promoter, or specialist co-op when you survey a thing.

!   Model: In the event that a blogger gets a PC from a producer to survey and will keep it, the person should disclose that reality.

!   In the event that you got an item with the expectation of complimentary you should unveil this data.

!   Any individual who is straightforwardly remunerated to expound on an item by an

publicist is covered by the new FTC rules.
Before I leave the subject of blog surveys, I might want to suggest that you truly consider doing video audits of the items you are assessing and add them to your survey webpage.

Video plain and just proselytes.

Making a Basic Video Bundle

The Workmanship and Business of Member Showcasing (Affiliate marketing)

One more extraordinary method for adapting your site is by making an exceptionally basic video bundle and afterward utilizing it to direct people to your press page and part with it.

These recordings are extremely easy to make and should be possible utilizing exceptionally straightforward instruments and hardware, for example, a computerized camera with video capacities or a Flip Video that you can get for close to $100-$130.

This cycle includes finding 10-20 inquiries that individuals are posing to in a productive Specialty of your decision.

There are numerous ways of tracking down these inquiries in the event that you can't concoct them all alone.

The following are a couple of ideas.

! Look into discussions inside the Specialty and figure out the thing questions individuals are inquiring.

o On the off chance that you are not finding question being asked you should simply make a post and ask individuals to post the top inquiries they have on the subject you are working with.

! Look at social destinations like Twitter and Facbook.

o Again same thing applies similarly as with the gathering. In the event that you see no one getting clarification on some pressing issues, ask them.

! Check Yippee replies.

! Do a quest on Google for the best 10 inquiries posed to on your point or the main 10 hints regarding your matter on the off chance that you are doing a top tips series.

! In the event that you have a rundown, do a review and inquire.

! Compose a post on your blog requesting individuals to leave you the inquiries they

have regarding your matter.

! Go to reside disconnected occasions as this is an incredible spot to get eye to eye video time.

! Go to other advertiser's live back and forth discussion calls and record the inquiries individuals are posing. This is likewise an extraordinary chance to record the response in the event that you, at the end of the day, don't have any idea.

! Watch your email. Commonly advertisers will convey messages subsequent to doing live calls telling you the top inquiries posed to by the participants.

!   Draw from your own insight and the inquiries you had when you initially began or that you have now.

Be imaginative the inquiries are out there being posed and they are very simple to find.

When you have your inquiries you are about to shoot a 3 brief video on each inquiry, and afterward supply the response.

Here are an ideal strides for you to follow:

1. Pick a Productive Specialty that you are proficient about or can research to track down the data.

2. Make 10-20 inquiries on the top inquiries individuals need to be aware of the Specialty you have picked. You might do the main 10 errors, or the best 10 issues, and so on...

3. Shoot short 3 brief recordings giving the issue and the arrangement. 1 video for every one of the 10-20

The Workmanship and Business of Member Showcasing (Affiliate marketing)

inquiries

!   Model: Hey this is Your Name from Your Area I'm a specialist Offer What Compels You The Master and I need to impart to you the main 10 inquiries and answer that individuals need to be familiar with Your Specialty . Offer Inquiry #1 And Give The Response To Address #1.

4. End your video with something like the accompanying model:

!   I have made a progression of these recordings that will truly assist with bouncing beginning your
Partner Showcasing Vocation. To get the whole 10 video set series of answers for the main 10 issues New Associate Advertisers are persistently tormented by go to Your Crush Page Space and I will send them right out to you.

5. Load every one of your recordings independently up to YouTube with a source of inspiration and connection guiding them back to your crush page.

Ensure your recordings are appropriately labeled utilizing the legitimate catchphrases being utilized to look for your subject you just made the recordings for. You need to get these recordings seen.

6. Next send them to your Crush page (or Blog) to pick in for the other 9 recordings in the series.

7. Pick a decent significant Member Item to send your new endorser of after they select in to your press page. When they pick in you will guide them to the business page of the Partner offer you have picked,

8. Pick an item with a decent changing over deals page and one that is straightforwardly connected with the Specialty you have picked and that will seem OK in the psyche of the supporter.

The following is the stream cycle of how this adaptation interaction will happen. Stage 1- Guest tracks down your video on YouTube

Stage 2-Guest is taken to your press page to get the whole video bundle you have made.

Stage 3-Guest is taken to a thank you page saying thanks to for picking in for the unconditional gift and guiding them to go to their email inbox and affirm that they truly do for sure need the unconditional gift.
Stage 4-Guest affirms by tapping on the connection in the email and is promptly taken to a deals page for the Partner item you have picked that is pertinent to the subject you made the recordings on.

This proposition will include more assistance the subject.

Stage 5-In the wake of buying the partner item the now purchaser is taken to the One Time Offer page of the Member item for an opportunity of you making more commissions.

There is another way you can move toward the adaptation cycle that might appear to be less agonizing for the guest to snatch the Offshoot item you have picked.

Stage 1-Guest tracks down your video on YouTube

Stage 2-Guest is taken to your press page to get the whole video bundle you have made.

Stage 3-Guest is taken to a thank you page saying thanks to for selecting in for the unconditional gift and guiding them to go to their email inbox and affirm that they really do for sure need the unconditional gift.

Stage 4-Guest is taken to the item download page where they will find an un-promoted reward hanging tight for them. This reward can be one more unconditional gift for them to join to that will lead them through your member connect to pursue the unconditional gift and squarely into the Item proprietor of the Associate item you have picked.

Utilizing Extra gives to upgrade Offshoot Item Proposals

One of the most amazing ways of upgrading any Associate item suggestion is to add unique extra proposals to the bundle.

The Workmanship and Business of Member Showcasing (Affiliate marketing)

In reality what we will be referring to is adding extra offers that make it simple for the guest to say OK since they will see more worth in the reward than the Associate item you are offering them.

Something you really want to remember all along is that the reward offer, Should Seem OK in the Brain of the Individual perusing The Proposition. You should constantly recollect this.

Commonly you will see extra offers that truly look bad with respect to why somebody would add them to an item proposal because of the reality they have no importance.

There are many advantages of adding extra gives to your proposals in the manner we will be examining.

! Benefits:

o Higher Transformation

o Gives You Greater Validity o Better Connections

o More Cash

o You Make An Item

Let me spread out the bit by bit configuration of utilizing a reward offer that appears to truly surpass the item you are suggesting, and that will assist you with capitalizing on your Subsidiary advancements.

1. Pick low end ($17-$67) territory Partner Item. Make progress toward supplanting this with your own item. You can track down these items in a few spots.

Recorded beneath are only 3 of the many spots for you to look.

!   ClickBank.com

!   CB Motor Track down ClickBank Commercial center Items that Sell.

Subsidiary advertising experts use CBEngine to investigate the top ClickBank Commercial center items to advance.

!   Pay Website . Com

2. Make Extreme Easy decision Reward Offer

!   My idea is a web-based studio; Find Private Name Privileges item in the Specialty that you have picked, and that will check out to turn into a reward, or make it from the substance of the Partner item you are advancing.

!   Make a 2-4 module Web based instructional class that will walk the client that purchases your Member item by the hand through the bit by bit course of learning the Specialty Point you are a Subsidiary for.

!   Note: Reward Offer needn't bother with to be totally prepared. It turns into an item that you will make as you go. You will convey this studio survive welcoming those that by the Offshoot item to make an appearance to your live studio preparation stages.

Obviously it is feasible to have this all around recorded so you can convey the studio using video accounts.

3. Compose an email and a blog entry that are basically the same in happy. The email you will convey on the very first moment of the advancement.

The blog entry will be where you will send them on day two of the advancement.

One choice to consider is the utilization of video on the blog rather composed content for higher change.

4. Start the advertising system by conveying the absolute first email.

The Workmanship and Business of Member Showcasing (Affiliate marketing)

This equivalent substance will be put on your blog either through composed content or video

When the guest peruses your email or your blog and taps on your member connect to buy the Subsidiary item, it is presently time to convey your guaranteed reward.

As coordinated in your email, the client will finish up a help ticket telling you they have bought by showing you're their buy receipt that they will get from the item proprietor of the Subsidiary item you are advancing

When you get the help ticket you will send back reorder guidelines guiding them to tap on the encased connection that will give them each of the headings they need to pursue the live studio reward, and when it will begin.

The connection they click on will lead them to a crush page to pursue the studio putting them on a rundown to assist you with speaking with the new purchasers.

Recall you don't have to begin the studio the following day.

You have some time. I would attempt to begin the studio inside a 7-multi day time frame to keep everybody amped up for joining in.

When the client pursues the studio they will start the twofold pick in course of affirming they to be sure need to get this data from you.

Obviously you know at this point that this is one more opportunity to adapt this interaction.

When they pick in they can be taken to a one time offer offering them an extraordinary chance to go to the studio, however to likewise possess the studio as their own personal top of the line instructional class after the studio is finished.

You might need to keep the instructional class locked down and simply offer exchange privileges to the item offering your clients the valuable chance to sell the item for you as opposed to guaranteeing it as their own.

One way or the other you have an incredible one time proposition to adapt your endeavors considerably further at a more exorbitant cost point than the first item you advanced.

The entire time the client is looking at your One Time Offer something mystical starts to happen directly in front of them that

will start an extraordinary relationship.

It is known as the subsequent email series.

When they twofold pick in to your rundown your absolute initially follow up email will be conveyed saying thanks to them for their buy and furthermore guiding them to look at the Subsidiary item they just bought from you.

Recollect your studio is being created around the Subsidiary item you elevated to them. You will be showing them the framework introduced in the item in more profundity than the actual item.

You believe that your client should begin going through the item so they can find out more about the techniques educated.

In this equivalent subsequent message you are giving the client affirmation that you will get with them in the following couple of days with more data about your live studio you are making.

The following stage in the process is to hold the live studio preparing.

The Workmanship and Business of Member Showcasing (Affiliate marketing)

My idea is to utilize Go to online course administration for setting your understudies on the call up to have the option to see you screen.

I would likewise utilize Camtasia to catch the recording of your studio.

Recollect this is turning into an item that you are assembling for you and conceivably for an OTO you just offered to your clients by offering them exchange or confidential mark freedoms to the preparation.

Ensure you record.

After every meeting of your studio you have a great chance to pursue those that poor person bought your One Time Deal to the bundle.

The explanation this is a particularly extraordinary opportunity to introduce your deal is on the grounds that those going to now see the nature of your preparation and what the nature of the item will be that they will claim or be selling.

They will know precisely exact thing they will get.

After your Preparation you actually have more chances to adapt this astonishing system.

Recollect the enchanted that started when your most memorable subsequent message went out.

Assuming you have taken care of your business appropriately you actually have more subsequent messages all set out that will keep on building your relationship with your new clients and furthermore advance related partner items you need to suggest.

Yet again you can take them right back through the entire cycle.

Complete Framework Totally Mechanized

This is an incredible framework however it requires a few endeavors and some work on your part. In any case, envision this framework totally computerized whenever you have accomplished the underlying work.

You know have an adaptation framework that will keep on getting you pay many days and a large number of months.

Each Time somebody makes an appearance to your site and they buy into your rundown they are conveyed this whole cycle starting with your Autoresponder Follow Up series!

When the interaction is finished it shoots the following item deal and rehashes a similar cycle.

When the subsequent cycle is finished, it shoots the following item deal and rehashes the interaction.

You set everything up by just reorder technique… you simply have to change the phrasing for the following item offer.

Do this process again… You simply direct people to your site.

Subsidiary Advertising Synopsis

!   Effective offshoots in any subsidiary program just don't stay there and trust that cash will come.

!   Why? There isn't any cash in that frame of mind around and pausing.

!   If you have any desire to find actual success in offshoot promoting and in the event that you need to constantly develop your subsidiary checks, you must follow through with something.

!   In particular have some good times being an Offshoot Advertiser. It's quite possibly of the best "plans of action" on the planet.

The Workmanship and Business of Member Showcasing (Affiliate marketing)

Advertising Outline

This book was gathered to give a nitty gritty casing of reference and guide your endeavors as you set out on making monetary freedom right from your own Home

You will be expected to work and keep on track.

This is all totally reachable and can change the direction of your life emphatically.

Both Kelvin and I have profited from the force of Showcasing On the web and we can guarantee you, on the off chance that you follow the means framed in this manual, you will make the truth of which dream and know is totally convince

Thank you for reading my ebook, please if u enjoy it kindly leave me a good comments on my page